W9-CIQ-365

How to Analyze the Films of

GEORGE
LUCAS

by Valerie Bodden

ABDO
Publishing Company

Essential Critiques

How to Analyze the Films of

GEORGE
LUCAS

by Valerie Bodden

Content Consultant: Michele Schreiber, PhD
assistant professor, Department of Film Studies, Emory University

Credits

Published by ABDO Publishing Company, 8000 West 78th Street, Edina, Minnesota 55439. Copyright © 2012 by Abdo Consulting Group, Inc. International copyrights reserved in all countries. No part of this book may be reproduced in any form without written permission from the publisher. The Essential Library™ is a trademark and logo of ABDO Publishing Company.

Printed in the United States of America,
North Mankato, Minnesota
062011
092011

Editor: Mari Kesselring
Copy Editor: Sarah Beckman
Interior Design and Production: Marie Tupy
Cover Design: Marie Tupy

Library of Congress Cataloging-in-Publication Data
Bodden, Valerie.
  How to analyze the films of George Lucas / by Valerie Bodden.
    p. cm. -- (Essential critiques)
  Includes bibliographical references and index.
  ISBN 978-1-61783-087-7
  1. Lucas, George, 1944---Criticism and interpretation--Juvenile literature. 2. Film criticism--Juvenile literature. I. Title.
  PN1998.3.L835B63 2011
  791.4302'33092--dc22
                                        2011006245

Table of Contents

Chapter

1

Introduction to Critiques

What Is Critical Theory?

What do you usually do as a member of an audience watching a movie? You probably enjoy the settings, the costumes, and the sound track. You learn about the characters as they are developed through dialogue and other interactions. You might be drawn in by the plot of the movie, eager to find out what happens next. Yet these are only a few of many ways of understanding and appreciating a movie. What if you are interested in delving more deeply? You might want to learn more about the director and how his or her personal background is reflected in the film. Or you might want to examine what the film says about society—how it depicts the roles of women and minorities, for example. If so, you have entered the realm of critical theory.

Critical theory helps you learn how various works of art, literature, music, theater, film, and other endeavors either support or challenge the way society behaves. Critical theory is the evaluation and interpretation of a work using different philosophies, or schools of thought. Critical theory can be used to understand all types of cultural productions.

There are many different critical theories. If you are analyzing a movie, each theory asks you to look at the work from a different perspective. Some theories address social issues, while others focus on the director's life, what role the direction plays in the overall film, or the time period in which the film was written or set. For example, the critical theory that asks how a director's life affected the work is called biographical criticism. Other common, broad schools of criticism include historical criticism, feminist criticism, auteur criticism, and ideological criticism.

What Is the Purpose of Critical Theory?

Critical theory can open your mind to new ways of thinking. It can help you evaluate a movie from a new perspective, directing your attention to issues and messages you may not otherwise recognize in a work. For example, applying feminist criticism to a film may make you aware of female stereotypes perpetuated in the work. Applying a critical theory to a work helps you learn about the person who created it or the society that enjoyed it. You can explore how the movie is perceived by current cultures.

How Do You Apply Critical Theory?

You conduct a critique when you use a critical theory to examine and question a work. The theory you choose is a lens through which you can view the work, or a springboard for asking questions about the work. Applying a critical theory helps you to think critically about the work. You are free to question the work and make an assertion about it. If you choose to examine a film using biographical criticism, for example, you want to know how the director's personal background inspired or shaped the work. You could explore why the director was drawn to the story. For instance, are there any parallels between a particular character's life and the director's life?

Forming a Thesis

Ask your question and find answers in the work or other related materials. Then you can create a thesis. The thesis is the key point in your critique. It is your argument about the work based on the tenets, or beliefs, of the theory you are using. For example, if you are using biographical criticism to ask how the director's life inspired the work, your thesis could be worded as follows: Director Teng Xiong, raised in refugee camps in Southeast Asia, drew upon her experiences to direct the movie, *No Home for Me*.

> ### How to Make a Thesis Statement
>
> In a critique, a thesis statement typically appears at the end of the introductory paragraph. It is usually only one sentence long and states the author's main idea.

Providing Evidence

Once you have formed a thesis, you must provide evidence to support it. Evidence might take the form of examples and quotations from the work itself—such as dialogue from a film. Articles about the movie or personal interviews with the director might also support your ideas. You may wish to address what other critics have written about the work. Quotes from these individuals may help support your claim. If you find any quotes or examples that contradict your thesis, you will need to create an argument against them.

For instance: <u>Many critics have pointed to the heroine of *No Home for Me* as a powerless victim of circumstances. However, through her dialogue and strong actions, she is clearly depicted as someone who seeks to shape her own future.</u>

How to Support a Thesis Statement

A critique should include several arguments. Arguments support a thesis claim. An argument is one or two sentences long and is supported by evidence from the work being discussed.

Organize the arguments into paragraphs. These paragraphs make up the body of the critique.

In This Book

In this book, you will read overviews of famous movies by director George Lucas, each followed by a critique. Each critique will use one theory and apply it to one work. Critical thinking sections will give you a chance to consider other theses and questions about the work. Did you agree with the author's application of the theory? What other questions are raised by the thesis and its arguments? You can also find out what other critics think about each particular film. Then, in the You Critique It section in the final pages of this book, you will have an opportunity to create your own critique.

> **Look for the Guides**
>
> Throughout the chapters that analyze the works, thesis statements have been highlighted. The box next to the thesis helps explain what questions are being raised about the work. Supporting arguments have been underlined. The boxes next to the arguments help explain how these points support the thesis. Look for these guides throughout each critique.

George Lucas has become one of the biggest names in Hollywood.

2

A Closer Look at George Lucas

George Lucas did not grow up planning to become famous. He did not even grow up planning to make movies. Instead, he wanted to drive race cars. But a near-fatal crash days before his high school graduation changed everything for Lucas. "That's when I decided . . . to try to do something with myself," Lucas later said.[1]

Born in Modesto

George Lucas was born in Modesto, California, on May 14, 1944. His mother, Dorothy, was often sick with stomach problems, so George and his three sisters were raised with the help of the family housekeeper, Till. George's father, George Sr., owned a stationery store. From a young age, George was a comic book fan, and when he was ten years old, his father bought the family's first television. George spent hours watching adventure shows.

While television and comics could hold his attention, school could not. George was a poor student. At the age of 16, he got his driver's license and began spending his nights cruising Modesto. On June 12, 1962, just three days before his high school graduation, George was in a horrendous car accident. As his car flipped, he was ejected from it. He suffered crushed lungs and several broken bones.

Getting Serious

During the long recovery period following his accident, Lucas decided that it was time to get serious about his future. He enrolled in Modesto Junior College, studying sociology, anthropology, literature, and creative writing. After graduating in 1964, he was accepted into the University of Southern California (USC) film school, where he at last discovered his true passion for making movies.

Lucas wrote and directed a number of student films, including *Electronic Labyrinth: THX 1138 4EB*, *Herbie*, and *Anyone Lived in a Pretty How Town*. *Electronic Labyrinth: THX 1138 4EB* won several awards, including first prize at the National Student Film Festival in 1968. During this time, Lucas also met Marcia Griffin, who would become his wife in 1969.

First Features

Lucas's first feature-length movie *THX 1138* (adapted from his shorter student film) opened in 1971. The bleak movie, which portrays a computer-controlled world in which humans are kept constantly sedated, received mixed reviews, leaving audiences feeling that he was a mechanical, humorless filmmaker. Lucas combated that image with his next film, *American Graffiti* (1973), a lighthearted story based in part on his own memories of nights spent cruising Modesto and set to a sound track of 1950s and 1960s rock-and-roll music. A hit with audiences and critics alike, the movie was nominated for five Academy Awards. Lucas, who had barely a penny to his name by the time the movie was finished, suddenly became a millionaire. As would become his custom, he shared some of his profits from the movie with key cast and crew members. He also bought a large house in San Anselmo, California, to serve as headquarters for Lucasfilm, the film production company he had founded in 1971.

The *Star Wars* Sensation

Despite the success of *American Graffiti*, two Hollywood studios rejected Lucas's next project, a science fantasy called *Star Wars*. Finally, Twentieth Century-Fox Film Corporation agreed to produce the film, and Lucas spent more than two years writing and revising a screenplay. The script called for a number of never-before-seen visual effects. Lucas formed his own special-effects workshop, called Industrial Light & Magic. From March 1976 until April 1977, Lucas spent nearly every waking moment directing and editing the movie. The hard work paid off. Within a week of its May 25, 1977, opening, *Star Wars* had grossed $2.89 million at the box office. The film was nominated for ten Academy Awards, taking home Oscars for art direction-set decoration, film editing, music-original score, sound, costume design, and visual effects.

Although pleased with the success of *Star Wars* and eager to make a sequel, Lucas was ready to step back from the exhausting role of director. He fleshed out the stories for the next two *Star Wars*

Lucas directed the first of his popular films in the 1970s.

movies—*The Empire Strikes Back* (1980) and *Return of the Jedi* (1983). But he ultimately served as executive producer, hiring others to develop the scripts and direct the final films. Both were huge successes.

Family Life

The financial success of the *Star Wars* movies allowed Lucas to purchase land in Marin County, California, where he established Skywalker Ranch to serve as a space where he and other directors could write and edit their movies. In 1981, he and his wife adopted a baby named Amanda. After the couple divorced in 1983, Amanda spent much of her time with Lucas. In 1988, Lucas adopted a second daughter, Katie, as a single father. In 1993, he added a son named Jett to the family.

Although he was no longer directing movies, Lucas served as executive producer on a number of films, including three *Indiana Jones* adventures: *Raiders of the Lost Ark* (1981), *Indiana Jones and the Temple of Doom* (1984), and *Indiana Jones and the Last Crusade* (1989), for which he had come up with the story idea. He was also executive producer of *Howard the Duck* (1986), *Willow* (1988), and *The Land Before Time* (1988).

Back in the Director's Chair

By the mid-1990s, Lucas was ready to return to the director's chair. The project would be one that he would always hold close to his heart—a prequel trilogy to the original *Star Wars* movies. The first movie, *The Phantom Menace* (1999), was a breakthrough in special effects technology. It includes a race scene generated almost entirely by

computer, as well as the all-digital character—Jar
Jar Binks. In the early years of the new millennium,
Lucas directed two more films for the prequel
trilogy, *Attack of the Clones* (2002) and *Revenge
of the Sith* (2005), making another breakthrough
by foregoing film to shoot these movies in digital
format.

Even with the *Star Wars* prequel under his
belt, Lucas was not yet ready to retire. He served
as executive producer on *Indiana Jones and the
Kingdom of the Crystal Skull* (2008) and *Red Tails*
(2010), based on his original story about African-
American pilots in World War II. Lucas's myriad
contributions to the movie world were recognized
with the Irving G. Thalberg Award in 1992, which
honors a "creative producer whose body of work
reflects a consistently high quality of motion-picture
production."[2] Despite the recognition and fame he
has earned, Lucas insists,

> *I didn't get into the movie business with
> any anticipation of becoming famous. It
> happened despite my best efforts, and it's
> something I don't really want. It's something
> I have to go through, but ultimately I'm just
> someone who makes movies.*[3]

Heroes and villains in *Star Wars* fight with lightsabers.

3

An Overview of
Star Wars: Episode IV A New Hope

Called simply *Star Wars* when it was first released in 1977, Lucas's first film in his epic space drama was re-titled *Episode IV A New Hope* in 1981 when *Episode V* was released. Although it was the first *Star Wars* film to be made, the title *Episode IV* reflected Lucas's plan to eventually make a prequel trilogy.

The movie opens with the now-famous words printed on the screen: "A long time ago in a galaxy far, far away."[1] Further words scrolling up the screen inform the audience of the situation. It is a period of civil war between the Galactic Empire and the Rebel Alliance. The rebel leader Princess Leia is attempting to smuggle plans for the Empire's Death Star to the rebel base. As her ship speeds through space, it is pursued by the Empire's Imperial forces.

A Plea for Help

Leia's ship is soon overtaken, and Imperial stormtroopers board the ship. They open fire on the Alliance soldiers. During the battle, Leia manages to hide in another part of the ship, where she programs the cylindrical droid (robot) R2-D2 with the Death Star's plans before being captured by stormtroopers, who bring her to Darth Vader. When she refuses to tell him the location of the rebel base, Darth Vader takes Leia prisoner on the Death Star.

Meanwhile, R2-D2 and another, more human-looking droid named C-3PO escape to the desert planet Tatooine. There, they are captured by aliens called Jawas, who sell them to Owen Lars. Lars's nephew, Luke Skywalker, is cleaning R2-D2 when he discovers a message from Leia: "Help me, Obi-Wan Kenobi, you're my only hope."[2] Intrigued, Luke asks his aunt and uncle about Obi-Wan, wondering if he might be his neighbor Ben Kenobi. When R2-D2 escapes in search of Obi-Wan, Luke follows and meets Obi-Wan, who tells him that he was a Jedi knight with Luke's father. Obi-Wan explains that the Jedi were once the guardians of peace in the galaxy and that they rely on an energy field called the Force for their power. He tells Luke that Luke's father was murdered by Darth Vader, who was seduced by the dark side of the Force, and offers to train Luke to be a Jedi. Luke refuses out of a sense of obligation to his aunt and uncle.

However, Luke returns home to find that his aunt and uncle have been murdered by stormtroopers. He decides to join Obi-Wan. The two travel to the spaceport of Mos Eisley, where they hire the renegade Han Solo and his first mate Chewbacca, an alien called a Wookiee, to fly them to Alderaan on Han's ship, the *Millennium Falcon*.

Aboard the Death Star, Leia is interrogated. When she still refuses to divulge the location of the rebel base, Grand Moff Tarkin, an Imperial governor, threatens to blow up Leia's home planet of Alderaan. Leia finally says that the base is on Dantooine (actually a former base), but Tarkin orders that Alderaan be blown up anyway. As a result, when the rescue team arrives at Alderaan, they find nothing but chunks of rock. They also see what they think is a moon but soon realize it is a space station. Suddenly, they are pulled in by the Death Star's tractor beam, a type of force field. Once aboard the Death Star, Obi-Wan sets out to turn off the tractor beam, while Luke, Han, and Chewbacca attempt to rescue Leia. Sensing a disturbance in the Force, Darth Vader realizes that Obi-Wan is aboard and sets out to find him, while Leia and her rescuers battle stormtroopers. Leia takes Luke's blaster gun and shoots a hole into a wall. The group plunges into a garbage compactor, and the walls begin to close in. However, Luke is able to communicate with C-3P0, who instructs R2-D2 to shut down the compactor.

The group emerges to fight more stormtroopers. Meanwhile, Obi-Wan has shut down the tractor beam and is now confronted by Darth Vader. As the two battle, Obi-Wan tells him, "If you strike me down, I shall become more powerful than you can possibly imagine."[3] As the others watch, Obi-Wan allows Darth Vader to strike him down, but rather than falling to the ground, Obi-Wan's body disappears. Suddenly, Luke hears Obi-Wan's voice through the Force, telling him to run. He and the others make their escape on the *Millennium Falcon*.

Destroying the Death Star

When the *Millennium Falcon* reaches the rebel base on the moon Yavin IV, the rebels come up with an attack plan. Since the Death Star was designed

Obi-Wan and Darth Vader battle with lightsabers.

to fight large ships, they decide to attack it with small, one-man fighters. As Luke and the rebel pilots prepare to take off, Han leaves, saying that his reward will not do him any good if he's dead.

As the pilots approach the Death Star, many are shot down. Luke remains, pursued by Darth Vader. Suddenly, Luke hears Obi-Wan telling him to use the Force. Luke turns off his targeting computer and prepares to fire. Meanwhile, Darth Vader has gained on Luke and is about to shoot him when Han appears in the *Millennium Falcon* and attacks Darth Vader, sending him careening into space. Luke fires, and the Death Star explodes. The movie concludes with Leia presenting Luke and Han with medals at an elaborate awards ceremony.

The depiction of Princess Leia in *A New Hope* reveals the changing attitudes about women in the 1970s.

4

How to Apply Historical Criticism to *Star Wars: Episode IV A New Hope*

What Is Historical Criticism?

Historical criticism looks at a work of art in the context of history. This school of criticism assumes that *when* a work was created has an influence on *what* the work portrays.

In order to examine a work from the perspective of historical criticism, a critic must first research and understand what was happening in the world when the work was created. The critic might discover connections between events, conditions, and attitudes in the real world and those portrayed in the work. Or he or she might find that the work is a reaction against the times. In either case, understanding the historical circumstances behind a work can help provide a deeper understanding of the work itself.

Applying Historical Criticism to *A New Hope*

When it was released in 1977, *Star Wars* created a sensation. It seemed to present a completely new world—filled with new planets, new spaceships, and new creatures. Yet, even this fantastical world held traces of contemporary American life, from the domination of white males to the fear of an evil empire and cold, soulless technology. Although it is set "a long time ago in a galaxy far, far away," *A New Hope* is both a reflection of and a reaction to US culture and social circumstances in the late 1970s.

The film reflects representations of and attitudes toward women and minorities common in US society in the late 1970s. In the late 1960s, the women's liberation movement, also known as second wave feminism, gained momentum. Women demanded equal opportunities and pay as their male counterparts. However,

> **Thesis Statement**
> The author presents the thesis statement in the first paragraph: "Although it is set 'a long time ago in a galaxy far, far away,' *A New Hope* is both a reflection of and a reaction to US culture and social circumstances in the late 1970s." The rest of the critique will present arguments to prove this thesis.

> **Argument One**
> This is the first argument: "The film reflects representations of and attitudes toward women and minorities common in US society in the late 1970s." The author will use historical research as well as evidence from the movie to support this point.

even as more women entered the workplace in the 1970s, females earned only approximately 60¢ for every dollar earned by white males. Yet, women continued to fight these trends and began to make inroads into traditionally male-dominated fields, including the military, with the first female pilots graduating from United States Air Force pilot training in 1977.

In this gender-charged atmosphere, Princess Leia—the only prominent female character of *A New Hope*—served as a reflection and role model for a generation of US women looking to break down the remaining gender barriers. Although she is a princess, Leia is not a traditional damsel in distress waiting for her hero. She participates in her own "rescue," taking charge and grabbing Luke's blaster to shoot a hole in the wall so the group can flee an attack by Imperial stormtroopers, saying, "Somebody has to save our skins."[1] After the group escapes from being almost crushed to death in the garbage compactor she has led them into, Han Solo lets Leia know what he thinks of her plan: "If we can just avoid any more female advice, we ought to be able to get out of here."[2] Although his emphasis on her advice being "female"—and, by implication,

Luke and Leia wear mostly white throughout the film.

inferior—reflects the attitude of many males in the workplace of the late 1970s, who were dealing with females in their profession for the first time, Leia is not intimidated. She puts Han in his place, telling him, "From now on, you do as I tell you."[3]

Like women, minorities of the late 1970s earned less than white males and held fewer positions of power. Unlike the powerful woman role model it presented in Leia, however, *A New Hope* offers no prominent minority characters. However, the aliens in the movie serve as representative of minorities. But the view that emerges is not positive. Aliens appear only on Tatooine, a planet on the fringes of the galaxy. Aside from the thieving Jawas and the vicious Sand People who roam the Tatooine desert, aliens are relegated to the cantina at the spaceport Mos Eisley, a city Obi-Wan refers to as a "wretched hive of scum and villainy," and many of the characters there appear to be less than savory.[4] This view of minorities as living in ghettos, immersed in lives of crime, reflects stereotypes common in films of the 1970s.

Additionally, the evil Darth Vader is presented in a black costume, versus Luke and Leia who wear mostly white throughout the film. Furthermore, Darth Vader's voice is supplied by an African American—James Earl Jones. This sets up a dichotomy of the "good guys" wearing white, while the "dark side" is covered in black and reinforces negative, racist stereotypes of African Americans.

Gender and race issues were not the only way in which *A New Hope* mirrored contemporary American life. Reflecting the United States' Cold War fear of the Soviet Union, the movie

> **Argument Two**
>
> In the second argument, the author asserts, "Reflecting the United States' Cold War fear of the Soviet Union, the movie presents an evil, soulless empire bent on using destructive technology to control the galaxy." This paragraph will compare the American views of the Soviet Union to the film's portrayal of the Galactic Empire.

presents an evil, soulless empire bent on using destructive technology to control the galaxy. By the time *A New Hope* was released in 1977, Americans had lived through three decades of the Cold War and fear of the rival Soviet Union, which many Americans saw as an "evil empire." This view is clearly reflected in *A New Hope*, where the Galactic Empire represents pure evil, and its minions, the stormtroopers, are faceless and undifferentiated, simple pawns to do the Empire's bidding.

In addition, the Empire relies on the destructive technology of the Death Star, a space station capable of destroying an entire planet. The Death Star's capability echoes that of the nuclear weapons that the United States and Soviet Union stockpiled throughout the Cold War—and that made each power capable of destroying the other many times over. Because of its reliance on technology, the Empire has become dehumanized, represented best, perhaps, by Darth Vader, who, with his black body armor and mechanical breathing, is more machine than man.

Yet, even with all of its technology, the Empire is unable to stand up against the Rebel Alliance, as Luke ultimately destroys the Death Star, winning

The Death Star is one of the Empire's weapons.

the battle. <u>With this victory, Americans demoralized by war, scandal, and economic recession were given a new hero—and "A New Hope."</u> Only four years before *A New Hope* reached theaters, the United States had pulled out of Vietnam, and Americans

Argument Three

In the third argument, the author shows how *A New Hope* was a reaction to conditions in the United States: "With this victory, Americans demoralized by war, scandal, and economic recession were given a new hero—and 'A New Hope.'"

remained disillusioned by a war that had no clear victor. The country had also been disheartened by the Watergate political scandal, rising inflation, high oil prices, and gas shortages. As public confidence in the US government was shaken, Luke's defeat of the Empire seemed to reassert the power of the individual. And his reliance on the Force rather than his targeting computer reinforced the idea that the solution to humankind's problems would be found in people, not detached, dehumanizing technology. Ultimately, the movie reassured viewers that good would ultimately triumph over evil—a concept absent from many of the period's films.

Conclusion
The final paragraph is the conclusion. The critique's main points are summarized, and the thesis, which has now been supported with evidence, is restated in part.

It is this timeless message of good triumphing over evil that has enabled *A New Hope* to resonate with audiences for more than 30 years. But even if its message defies a specific time period, the film's characterization of women and minorities, representation of an evil empire, and presentation of a new hero offer a glimpse of the culture and conditions of 1970s America. Perhaps it was not such a long time ago—and maybe the galaxy was not so very far away.

Thinking Critically about *A New Hope*

Now it is your turn to assess the critique. Consider these questions:

1. The thesis emphasizes that *A New Hope* offers a view of 1970s American life. Do you agree? Why or why not?

2. The author argues that Luke's triumph over evil offered a new hero to people of the 1970s. Does Luke's heroism speak to today's generation as well? If yes, how so?

3. This critique portrays Leia as a role model for young women of the 1970s. Can Leia still be seen as a role model for today's young women, or is her position outdated?

4. The author argues that technology, such as the Death Star, is presented as dangerous and negative in the film, reflecting the era's opinion of such tools. How might an audience today perceive technology in the film?

Other Approaches

What you have just read is one possible way to apply historical criticism to the film *A New Hope*. What are some other ways to apply this approach? Remember that historical criticism examines a work in the context of when it was created. Following are two alternate approaches.

The Global Economy

Author Carl Silvio argues that *Star Wars* was released during America's transition from an economy based on mass production to one based on information technology, specialized jobs, and a global marketplace. He points to the intergalactic nature of the Mos Eisley spaceport as evidence of this new economy and sees the movie's technology as representing "the sense of wonder and fear that we feel when confronting global capitalism."[5]

The thesis statement for such a critique could be: Through its portrayal of advanced technologies and the interaction of alien races from across the galaxy, *A New Hope* reflected the United States' transition from a production economy to a global, information-based economy.

Humanizing Technology

Some critics argue that *Star Wars* humanizes and glorifies technology. The droids C-3PO and R2-D2, for example, have many human characteristics. The movie's presentation of technology came at a time when technology in the real world was developing rapidly, with the appearance of personal computers, VCRs, and America's first space station.

The thesis statement for such a critique could be: Through its presentation of humanized technology, *A New Hope* glorifies the technological achievements of the 1970s.

Qui-Gon Jinn, *left*, and Obi-Wan Kenobi battle Darth Maul, *center*.

5

An Overview of
Star Wars: Episode I
The Phantom Menace

More than 20 years after the original *Star Wars* hit
theaters, Lucas returned to the saga. He released
Star Wars: Episode I The Phantom Menace in 1999.
This film takes place 32 years before the events of
A New Hope. Whereas the original *Star Wars* trilogy
tells the story of Luke Skywalker, the prequel
trilogy focuses on his father, Anakin Skywalker—
or, as he is later known, Darth Vader.

Like all of the *Star Wars* movies, *The Phantom
Menace* opens with a prelude text scrolling up the
screen. The text reports that the Galactic Republic is
in disarray and that the Trade Federation has set up
a blockade of battleships around the planet Naboo.
In an attempt to resolve the dispute, Supreme
Chancellor Valorum (leader of the Galactic
Republic's Senate) has sent two Jedi knights,

Qui-Gon Jinn and Obi-Wan Kenobi, to a Trade
Federation ship to negotiate.

The Planet Naboo

When the Trade Federation's Viceroy Nute
Gunray learns of the presence of Jedi on his ship,
he is terrified and consults via hologram with a
mysterious cloaked figure named Darth Sidious, a
Sith Lord (someone who relies on the dark side of
the Force). Darth Sidious instructs Gunray to kill
the Jedi and begin an invasion of Naboo. Although
droids are sent to kill Qui-Gon and Obi-Wan, the
two Jedi stow aboard landing craft and escape
to Naboo, where Qui-Gon saves Jar Jar Binks, a
member of the Gungans (an alien species that lives
in underwater cities). Qui-Gon, Obi-Wan, and Jar
Jar make a perilous trip through the planet's core to
reach Naboo's capital of Theed.

Meanwhile, Trade Federation forces capture
Queen Amidala, leader of the Naboo, along with her
handmaidens. Among the handmaidens is Padmé,
whom we later learn is the real queen in disguise.
(The queen in royal attire in many—but not all—
scenes is actually a decoy meant to keep the real
queen safe.) As the droids lead Padmé, the decoy

Young Anakin
Skywalker

queen, and the other handmaidens out of the palace,
Qui-Gon and Obi-Wan make a surprise attack,
destroying the droids and freeing the queen and
the others. Afterward, the queen decides to travel
to Coruscant to plead with the Senate to end the
Trade Federation's invasion. As Padmé, along with
her decoy and the Jedi, fly through the Federation's
blockade, their ship is damaged, and they stop on
the desert planet Tatooine for repairs.

Meeting Anakin Skywalker

On Tatooine, Padmé accompanies Qui-Gon, Jar
Jar, and R2-D2 to the spaceport Mos Espa. There,
the three meet nine-year-old Anakin Skywalker,

a slave of the junk dealer Watto. With a sandstorm approaching, Anakin invites Qui-Gon, Padmé, R2-D2, and Jar Jar to take shelter at his house. He promises them that if he wins the upcoming Boonta Eve pod race, he will give them his winnings to buy the parts they need for their ship.

Qui-Gon, who recognizes that the Force is unusually strong in Anakin, sends a blood sample from the boy to Obi-Wan, who analyzes it and discovers that Anakin's midi-chlorian count is off the charts. (Qui-Gon later explains that midi-chlorians are life forms found in living cells that can tell Jedi the will of the Force.) Recognizing the boy's potential, Qui-Gon makes a bet with Watto—if Anakin wins the race, he will be free. Anakin does win the race, and he leaves his mother to go with the others to Coruscant. Just as they are about to board their ship, however, they are attacked by Darth Maul, whom Darth Sidious had sent to kill the queen. They escape unscathed.

The Senate and the Jedi Council

When the group arrives on Coruscant, the queen is greeted by Naboo's Senator Palpatine, who warns her that the Senate is not likely to take any action on Naboo's behalf. He suggests that she call for a vote of no confidence in Chancellor Valorum so that a new, stronger chancellor can be elected. When Queen Amidala presents her case to the Senate, charging the Trade Federation with invading her planet, she is asked to defer her request so that a commission can be established to investigate the charges. Refusing, she calls for a vote of no confidence in the chancellor, and Senator Palpatine is nominated to take his place.

Meanwhile, Qui-Gon brings Anakin before the Jedi Council, which recognizes that the Force is strong in the boy. Yet, the Jedi masters say that Anakin is too old to begin Jedi training. In addition, Yoda senses much fear in the boy and warns that "fear leads to anger; anger leads to hate; hate leads to suffering."[1] Qui-Gon, however, insists that Anakin is the chosen one, referring to an ancient prophecy about a chosen one who will restore balance to the Force.

Battle on Naboo

Realizing that the Senate will be no help to her people, Queen Amidala decides to return to her home planet. She is once again accompanied by

Qui-Gon, Obi-Wan, Anakin, and Jar Jar. As soon as they arrive on Naboo, Jar Jar leads the group to the Gungans, where they meet with Gungan leader Boss Nass. As the decoy queen begins to speak to him, Padmé steps forward and confesses her true identity, then kneels and begs the Gungans for their help, which they agree to give.

As the Gungans battle the droid army in the countryside, Padmé leads the Jedi and her security forces into the capital city. There, the pilots will try to disable the droid control ship. Anakin jumps into a ship for safety. As Qui-Gon and Obi-Wan confront Darth Maul in a lightsaber battle, Anakin attempts to fire on droids in the hangar but accidentally takes off.

Padmé and her security forces head for the throne room, battling the Federation's droids along the way. Eventually, the droids surround Padmé and her guards, and they are forced to surrender. As they are taken into the throne room to see Viceroy Gunray, the decoy queen approaches, and, believing her to be the real queen, the viceroy orders his droids after her, allowing Padmé and her men to take the viceroy prisoner.

Meanwhile, Anakin reaches the droid control ship, which he blows up by accident. The droids

fighting the Gungans lose power and are suddenly
motionless. At the palace, Obi-Wan continues to
battle Darth Maul, who has stabbed Qui-Gon with
his lightsaber. Obi-Wan kills Darth Maul and then
runs to Qui-Gon, who asks him to promise to train
Anakin. As Obi-Wan agrees to train Anakin, Qui-
Gon dies. Later, Obi-Wan speaks to Yoda, who
ultimately allows Obi-Wan to take Anakin as an
apprentice. After a solemn funeral ceremony for
Qui-Gon, punctuated by Yoda's fears that the Sith,
long believed to be extinct, are still alive, the movie
ends on a bright note, with a victory celebration.

The droid army

By applying feminist criticism to *The Phantom Menace*, you can look at how the film portrays women such as Queen Amidala, *left*, compared with Jar Jar Binks, *right*.

6

How to Apply Feminist Criticism to *Star Wars: Episode I The Phantom Menace*

What Is Feminist Criticism?

Feminism is the belief that women's rights and opportunities should be equal to those of men. Feminist criticism, therefore, looks at the way a work of art portrays women and women's rights. When analyzing a work from the perspective of feminism, a critic might examine what kinds of roles female characters are assigned. Are women in positions of power, making their own intelligent decisions? Or are they inferior, reporting to and acting on the demands of a male authority? The answer to these questions can help the critic determine whether the work presents stereotypical images of women as caretakers, beauty objects, or damsels needing protection, or if it throws off those stereotypes to show women as equal to men.

Applying Feminist Criticism to
The Phantom Menace

The world of *Star Wars: Episode I The Phantom Menace* is dominated by males. Nearly all power is in the hands of the Jedi Council and the Galactic Senate, both of which are made up mostly of males. In fact, the only prominent female characters in the movie are Queen Amidala, leader of the Naboo people, and her decoy. Far from being overshadowed by the men in her world, however, Queen Amidala emerges as a powerful leader. At the same time, she remains a caring and compassionate woman. The character of Queen Amidala proves that women can be strong, courageous, and intelligent leaders without sacrificing their femininity.

Thesis Statement

This thesis statement addresses the issue of how a woman leader is presented in this film: "The character of Queen Amidala proves that women can be strong, courageous, and intelligent leaders without sacrificing their femininity."

As *The Phantom Menace* opens, Naboo has been invaded by the Trade Federation, whose leaders are attempting to force Queen Amidala to sign a treaty legalizing the Federation's invasion. Darth Sidious, a Sith Lord who has secretly instigated the invasion, assures the Federation's

Viceroy Nute Gunray that he will have no trouble with the queen: "Queen Amidala is young and naïve. You will find controlling her will not be difficult."[1] But Darth Sidious is wrong. <u>The queen proves to be a strong and decisive leader.</u> She does not sign the treaty even after being captured by the Trade Federation, and she later pleads her people's case before the Galactic Senate. There, she refuses to wait for a Senate commission to investigate her charge, forcefully declaring, "I've come before you to resolve this attack on our sovereignty now. I was not elected to watch my people suffer and die while you discuss this invasion in a committee."[2]

Argument One

The author gives the first argument in support of the thesis: "The queen proves to be a strong and decisive leader."

While making tough decisions on behalf of her people, Queen Amidala is willing to risk her personal safety. <u>Far from a damsel in distress, the queen is as brave as any of the men assigned to protect her.</u> She shows no signs of weakness or fear at the Mos Espa spaceport on Tatooine. Later, back on Naboo, the queen

Argument Two

The author asserts that the queen is not a "damsel in distress," but a courageous leader.

shows no fear when it comes time to capture the viceroy and retake the capital city. Throughout the battle, she is at the head of her security forces, leading the men through the palace halls toward the throne room and firing at the Federation's droids along the way.

Queen Amidala is not only courageous in battle, but also intelligent. It is her idea to approach the Gungans to request help in defeating the Federation. Although Qui-Gon expresses his doubts that the Gungans can be convinced and acknowledges that he and Obi-Wan will be unable to help, the queen goes forward with her plan. Knowing that the Gungans believe the Naboo feel superior, the queen first reveals her true identity to them—dressed more like a commoner than royalty—and then kneels before them in an act of humility that persuades them to join the fight. Still, the men with her are not convinced that the addition of the Gungans will make a difference against the Federation's powerful droid army. The queen then reveals her master plan: the battle is a diversion to draw the droids away from the city,

where the queen, her security forces, and the Jedi will take back the palace and capture the viceroy. The plan is well-conceived, Qui-Gon admits. Even Darth Sidious is shocked by the queen's boldness: "This is an unexpected move for her. It's too aggressive."[3]

Dressed as Padmé, the queen is still strong and courageous in battle.

    Even as she takes on the role of a powerful, intelligent, and courageous leader, Queen Amidala retains her characteristically "feminine" traits. She does not have to become masculine, mannish, or even "sexless" in order to exercise her power and strength.

> **Argument Four**
> In the fourth argument, the author demonstrates that although the queen is not a stereotypical female, she remains feminine.

Throughout the movie, the queen wears elaborate dresses and headpieces, and her face is very obviously made up. Even when disguised as Padmé, who dresses more plainly, the queen is still feminine, with her long hair clearly visible. It is not only her clothing that demonstrates the queen's femininity, but also her attitude. Unlike the males around her, who warn Anakin not to focus on how much he misses his mother, Padmé motherly comforts the young boy in his loneliness.

Conclusion
This final paragraph is the conclusion. It sums up the arguments presented in the critique and partially restates the thesis, which has now been backed up with evidence.

In the end, Queen Amidala's leadership frees her people from the tyranny of the Trade Federation. Newly elected Supreme Chancellor Palpatine praises the queen's leadership and affirms that it was she who brought an end to the invasion, saying, "Your boldness has saved our people, Your Majesty."[4] As for Darth Sidious, he now knows that Queen Amidala is a force to be reckoned with. She may be young and feminine, but that does not mean she is weak or easy to control. Quite the opposite: she is a strong, courageous leader who is more than capable of handling whatever situation comes her way.

Thinking Critically about
The Phantom Menace

Now it is your turn to assess the critique. Consider these questions:

1. Do you agree with the author's thesis that Queen Amidala is strong, courageous, intelligent, and feminine all at the same time?

2. What was the strongest argument? What was the weakest? Could any other arguments have been made to support the thesis?

3. Based on this analysis, what message do you think the film sends about female leaders? Does it seem to say anything about male leaders?

Other Approaches

What you have just read is one possible way to apply feminist criticism to the film *The Phantom Menace*. What are some other ways to apply this approach? Remember that feminist criticism examines how a work portrays women. Following are two alternate approaches.

A Patriarchal Society

Some critics have argued that the world presented in the *Star Wars* movies is patriarchal— that is, ruled by men. Women are almost completely excluded from *The Phantom Menace*, aside from the queen, her handmaidens, and Anakin's mother. Nearly all of the Jedi we see in the movie are male, as are most of the leaders of the Senate.

A thesis statement for such a critique could be: The near-total exclusion of women from the world of *The Phantom Menace* reveals a patriarchal society in which women can have little power.

Amidala as a Weak Queen

Rather than seeing Queen Amidala as a strong leader, some viewers might interpret her actions as weak and indecisive. Although she disagrees with Qui-Gon's decision on Tatooine to entrust their fate to a bet made on a pod race, for example, Padmé does not assert her authority as the real queen. In addition, she allows herself to be manipulated by Senator Palpatine.

The thesis statement for such a critique could be: Although Queen Amidala is in a position of power, she frequently defers to and is even manipulated by the male authority figures who surround her.

In *Attack of the Clones*, Obi-Wan Kenobi, *right*, and Anakin Skywalker are in charge of protecting Padmé Amidala.

7

An Overview of
Star Wars: Episode II
Attack of the Clones

Attack of the Clones picks up ten years after
the end of *The Phantom Menace*. During those
ten years, the situation in the Galaxy has not
improved, and now thousands of solar systems
have joined a Separatist movement led by former
Jedi Count Dooku. With the Senate about to vote
on a militarization act authorizing the creation
of an army of the Republic, Naboo's former
queen, Padmé Amidala, now a senator, travels to
Coruscant.

Assassination Attempts

Moments after the senator's ship lands on
Coruscant, it explodes, killing her decoy. Padmé
herself was on a smaller ship and survives. As
a result of the attack, Padmé is placed under

the protection of Jedi Obi-Wan Kenobi and his padawan, or apprentice, Anakin Skywalker.

That night, Anakin and Obi-Wan talk outside of Amidala's room. She has covered the cameras— apparently uncomfortable with Anakin watching her—but the two suddenly sense danger in her room. They burst through the door, and Anakin kills two poisonous kouhuns (long, centipede-like creatures) crawling over the senator's bed. Obi-Wan leaps out the window to grab the droid that released the creatures. He hangs from the droid as it flies through the city but is eventually shot off of it and falls through a maze of flying ships before being caught by Anakin, who has leapt into a flying speeder car. The two chase down and capture the would-be assassin, but just as she is about to tell them the name of the bounty hunter who hired her, the assassin is shot with a poisonous dart and dies.

The Planets Kamino and Naboo

After the second attempt on Padmé's life, the Jedi Council assigns Obi-Wan to track down the bounty hunter behind the assassination attempt, while Anakin is to escort the senator back to Naboo. Aboard the ship to Naboo, Anakin and Padmé

discuss his life as a Jedi. When Padmé questions
whether Jedi are allowed to love, Anakin replies,
"Attachment is forbidden; possession is forbidden;
compassion, which I would define as unconditional
love, is central to a Jedi's life. So you might say that
we are encouraged to love."[1] On Naboo, Anakin
and Padmé kiss, although she draws away, saying
she should not have done it. The two spend much
time together, and Anakin eventually confesses his
love for her. Padmé, however, refuses to be swayed,
telling him that their roles as a senator and a Jedi
make a relationship impossible. Although Anakin
says they could keep their relationship a secret,
Padmé is unwilling to live a lie.

Meanwhile, Obi-Wan searches for the origin
of the dart that was used to kill Padmé's assassin.
He tracks it to Kamino, a planet of cloners. He
travels there and learns that the Kaminoans have
been making a clone army for the Republic. When
he reports this development to Jedi masters Yoda
and Mace Windu, they are shocked to realize that
an army could have been created without their
knowledge. Afterward, Obi-Wan pursues the bounty
hunter Jango Fett, whom he suspects of having
hired Padmé's assassin.

Seeking Revenge

On Naboo, Anakin confesses to Padmé that he has had a nightmare about his mother; she was suffering and in pain. He tells the senator that he must travel to Tatooine to rescue his mother, and Padmé offers to accompany him.

On Tatooine, Anakin learns that his mother has been captured by the planet's fierce Tusken Raiders. Leaving Padmé with his mother's husband, Cliegg Lars, Anakin speeds across the desert toward the Tuskens' camp.

At the camp, Anakin finds his mother inside a tent, tied up and bleeding. He unties her and speaks with her briefly before she dies in his arms. In rage, Anakin leaves the tent and kills the entire tribe of Tusken Raiders.

After bringing his mother's body back to her house, Anakin talks with Padmé. She attempts to console him, saying that he could not have prevented his mother's death because he is not all-powerful. But Anakin refuses to be comforted, saying, "Well, I should be. Someday I will be. I will be the most powerful Jedi ever. I promise you. I will even learn to stop people from dying."[2]

Battle of Geonosis

Meanwhile, Obi-Wan manages to track Jango
Fett to the planet Geonosis, where he follows him
into a droid factory set in underground caves.
There, he looks on as Count Dooku and Viceroy
Nute Gunray of the Trade Federation discuss
killing Senator Amidala. Unable to send a message
to Coruscant, Obi-Wan relays the news through
Anakin on Tatooine. Before he can complete his
transmission, he is attacked by battle droids and
captured by Count Dooku, who tells him that the
Senate is now under the control of the Dark Lord of
the Sith, a fact that Obi-Wan refuses to believe.

Back on Coruscant, Jar Jar Binks, who has
been appointed to stand as Naboo's senator during
Padmé's absence, proposes that the Senate grant
emergency powers to Chancellor Palpatine. The
powers are granted, and Palpatine makes his first
act the creation of an army.

On Geonosis, Anakin and Padmé—who have
traveled from Tatooine to rescue Obi-Wan—fall
onto a droid assembly line, where they must
dodge huge, pounding machines. They escape
the machines but are captured by droids. As they
are about to be led to their execution, Padmé

confesses her love for Anakin, and the two kiss.
They are led into a large arena, where Obi-Wan is
already chained to a tall post. Three large beasts are
unleashed to attack the three prisoners, but they all
manage to free themselves and escape the creatures.
They are not safe, however, as droids enter the
arena and surround them. Suddenly, Jedi throughout
the arena pull out lightsabers and begin slaying
droids. The Jedi are outnumbered, however, and
eventually a small group of survivors is surrounded
by the droids. Just as rescue appears hopeless,
several smaller ships carrying Yoda and the clone
army descend into the arena. The clones join the
Jedi, and the battle against the droids resumes.

As Dooku flees the battle, Obi-Wan, Anakin,
and Padmé pursue him, but Padmé falls out of
the ship along the way. Anakin demands that they
rescue her, but Obi-Wan insists that they do their
duty; Anakin reluctantly agrees. The two follow
Dooku into a cave, and Anakin rushes at him but is
knocked out by Dooku's Force Lightning (electric
bolts shot from the hands). Dooku and Obi-Wan
battle, and Anakin gets up just in time to keep
Dooku from killing Obi-Wan. Meanwhile, Padmé
rises from her fall and heads toward the transport

where Obi-Wan and Anakin are battling Dooku. During the fight, Dooku cuts off Anakin's arm. Before Dooku can flee, Yoda enters the cave. He and Dooku battle, but Dooku manages to escape. Dooku meets with Darth Sidious, who is pleased that everything is going according to plan.

Anakin and Padmé fall in love.

After returning to Coruscant, Yoda tells Obi-Wan that the battle was not a victory, for the Clone War has now begun. The movie concludes on faraway Naboo, where Anakin and Padmé are united in a secret wedding ceremony.

Anakin displays a developing moral ambivalence in *Attack of the Clones.*

How to Apply New Criticism to *Star Wars: Episode II Attack of the Clones*

What Is New Criticism?

New Criticism was developed in the 1920s, and since that time, it has become one of the predominant methods for critiquing a work of art. New Critics work under the premise that a work of art stands on its own and should by analyzed without regard to outside factors such as history, authorship, or even a reader's (or viewer's) response.

In order to evaluate a work on the basis of New Criticism, an author must conduct a "close reading" of the work. This means that he or she examines each of the various parts of a work—its characters, dialogue, action, and imagery. The critic's goal is to determine how these complex parts interact to create a unified work.

Applying New Criticism to *Attack of the Clones*

On the surface, *Star Wars: Episode II Attack of the Clones* seems to be a story of opposites—light and dark, good and evil, Jedi and Sith. A look beneath the surface, however, reveals that the division between good and evil is not as clear-cut as it first appears. A close reading of the dialogue, actions, and symbolic imagery of *Attack of the Clones* reveals a complex world in which moral certainty fades into moral ambivalence.

The Jedi, of course, represent the light, the good, the right path. The Sith, on the other hand, are tyrannical, bringing death and destruction as they use the dark side of the Force in their ruthless quest for power. Yet, the Sith are at times more honest than the Jedi. The Jedi-turned-Sith Count Dooku, for example, is being truthful when he tells Obi-Wan Kenobi that the Republic is "now under the control of the Dark

Thesis Statement

The author presents the thesis statement at the end of the introduction: "A close reading of the dialogue, actions, and symbolic imagery of *Attack of the Clones* reveals a complex world in which moral certainty fades into moral ambivalence."

Argument One

This is the author's first argument: "Yet, the Sith are at times more honest than the Jedi." The rest of this paragraph will provide examples to prove the argument.

Lord of the Sith. . . . Hundreds of Senators are now under the influence of a Sith Lord called Darth Sidious."[1] Although Dooku does not mention that he is working with Darth Sidious, he is honest with the Jedi about the Sith Lord. Obi-Wan, however, insists that if Sidious had infiltrated the Senate, the Jedi would have sensed it through the Force, to which Dooku offers another truth: "The dark side of the Force has clouded their vision, my friend."[2] In fact, the Jedi themselves realize that their ability to use the Force is weakening. After Obi-Wan discovers the clone army on Kamino, Yoda is shocked, telling Mace Windu, "Blind we are if creation of this clone army we could not see."[3] Yet, when Windu suggests that they inform the Senate of their diminishing ability, Yoda says they must keep this information to themselves. In his decision to commit a deliberate deception, Yoda slips from the light side of the Force.

In addition, the Jedi, who are meant to follow the way of peace and rely on the Force, turn to the darker powers of technology and aggression in their attempt to save the Republic. In his quest

> **Argument Two**
>
> The author begins this paragraph with the second argument: "In addition, the Jedi, who are meant to follow the way of peace and rely on the Force, turn to the darker powers of technology and aggression in their attempt to save the Republic."

to discover the origin of the dart used to execute Padmé's assassin, Obi-Wan's first instinct is to rely on analysis droids and computer archives, for which his friend, Dexter Jettster, reprimands him: "I should think that you Jedi would have more respect for the difference between knowledge and wisdom."[4] As they turn from the Force, the Jedi also begin to turn toward aggression. It is they—and not the Separatists—who are the aggressors in the battle on Geonosis. During the course of that battle, the Jedi are surrounded by Dooku's droids. But then Yoda arrives, bringing with him the clone army whose creation was earlier so reprehensible to him. Setting aside Mace Windu's earlier comment that the Jedi are "keepers of the peace, not soldiers," Yoda directs the clones into battle.[5] He has turned to both aggression and technology and in so doing has taken further steps away from the light side.

The fall of the Jedi into moral ambivalence is reflected especially in the storyline of Anakin Skywalker. Anakin is being trained in the light side of the Force, and he wants the same

Argument Three

In the third argument, the author shows how one character in particular falls into moral ambivalence: "The fall of the Jedi into moral ambivalence is reflected especially in the storyline of Anakin Skywalker."

things as the other Jedi want: to identify Padmé's would-be killer, to stop the Separatists, and to maintain peace and order in the galaxy. Yet, Anakin feels conflicted. He is grateful for the tutelage of Obi-Wan. But at the same time, he resents Obi-Wan for holding him back.

Yoda strays from the light side when he directs the clones into battle.

He wants to be fully committed to the Jedi order, which forbids attachment to another human being, but he also wants to have a romantic relationship with Padmé. In an attempt to have it both ways, Anakin slips into moral ambivalence and becomes willing to deceive, telling Padmé that they could have a secret relationship. Although Padmé at first refuses, the film concludes with the couple's secret marriage, bringing both further from the light side. During their wedding ceremony, we see that Anakin has also turned to technology, as his new, metallic hand grasps Padmé's human one. But Anakin's greatest fall away from the light side is seen in his turn to aggression as he slaughters the tribe of Tusken Raiders—"And not just the men, but the women and the children, too," as he tells Padmé—after his mother's death at their hands.[6] Yet, even here, Anakin is not fully evil, as he shows a degree of remorse for what he has done.

Throughout the film, symbolic imagery helps to reinforce the moral ambivalence that envelops Anakin and the Jedi. In several scenes, clouds and fog obscure the characters' vision, just as their view of how to follow the light side of the force has become obscured. In fact, the buildings in the Republic's capital of Coruscant, where the Jedi Council meets, reach all the way into the clouds. And a murky haze of dust and smoke envelops the battle on Geonosis, a battle that represents the Jedi's ultimate turn to aggression and technology.

Along with clouds and fog, symbolic colors help to reflect the protagonists' growing moral uncertainty. As Anakin tears across the desert on Tatooine in search of his mother, the sky is red, broken up by heavy, menacing clouds, foreshadowing Anakin's coming murderous anger. As the clones are loaded onto ships to depart from Coruscant at the end of the film, the sky is again red, since this army also represents aggression and bloodshed.

Finally, images of literal descent mirror the characters' moral descent throughout the film. Ships repeatedly descend onto planets, often through clouds or fog. Obi-Wan plunges from the droid that has attempted to assassinate Padmé and then later is left dangling from a bridge on Kamino. On Tatooine, Anakin jumps off a high, rocky cliff into the camp of the Tusken Raiders, and on Geonosis, both he and Padmé leap from a retracting bridge onto the assembly line of a droid factory. Not long afterward, the Jedi's moral compromise is made complete as the clones descend onto that planet.

Although the clones ultimately save the Jedi from being wiped out in the Battle of Geonosis, their arrival does not represent victory for the light side. Darth Sidious's chilling final comment that everything is going according to plan reveals that the Jedi have played right into his hands. Yoda, too, realizes now that the fall into moral ambivalence has strengthened the Jedi's adversaries: "The shroud of the Dark Side has fallen. Begun the Clone War has."[7]

> **Conclusion**
> The final paragraph concludes the critique by summing up the arguments and partially restating the thesis, which has now been backed up with evidence.

Thinking Critically About *Attack of the Clones*

Now it is your turn to assess the critique. Consider these questions:

1. Do you agree that the line between good and evil in *Attack of the Clones* is blurred? Where do you see a clear division between the two sides? Where is the division less clear?

2. Which of the arguments was most convincing? Which seemed weak? How could it be stronger?

3. Do you see any other symbolic imagery in this movie? What do you think it represents?

Other Approaches

What you have just read is one possible way to apply New Criticism to the film *Attack of the Clones*. What are some other ways to apply this approach? Remember that New Criticism looks only at the work being analyzed. Following are two alternate approaches.

Unity and the Force

Many critics see the Force as the ultimate unifying factor in the *Star Wars* universe. As author William O. Stephens contends, "How the Force is conceived, used, or ignored by the characters goes a long way to determining their identities, allegiances, and goals."[8]

The thesis statement for a critique that focuses on the use of the Force might be: Through their actions and dialogue, the characters in *Attack of the Clones* reveal how the Force controls—and is controlled by—those on both the light side and the dark side, ultimately unifying the galaxy and keeping it in balance.

A Sense of Confusion

Throughout much of this film, characters are confused by circumstances. They do not know who is trying to kill Padmé, why the clone army was ordered for the Republic, or what the Separatists are up to. This confusion is reflected in the film's complex plots, rapid-fire action, and doublespeak.

The thesis statement for such a critique could be: The film's complex, intertwining plots, rapid-fire action, and deceptive dialogue create a theme of confusion and mystery.

Revenge of the Sith hit theaters in 2005.

9

An Overview of
Star Wars: Episode III Revenge of the Sith

Revenge of the Sith, the final movie of the *Star Wars* prequel trilogy, opens three years after the beginning of the Clone Wars. War continues to rage between the Republic and the Separatists, who are led by Count Dooku, along now with General Grievous, the part-droid, part-alien commander of the Separatists' droid army. Grievous has captured Chancellor Palpatine, and Obi-Wan Kenobi and Anakin Skywalker have been dispatched to rescue the chancellor.

During the course of the rescue, the two Jedi battle Count Dooku. Anakin cuts off Dooku's hands and then, at the chancellor's urging, kills him. Afterward, he regrets what he has done, saying it is not the Jedi way, but Palpatine praises his action, saying, "It is only natural. He cut off your arm, and you wanted revenge."[1] Before escaping, Anakin stops to rescue Obi-Wan, who was knocked unconscious during the battle with Dooku, despite the fact that the chancellor urges him to leave his fellow Jedi and save himself.

The Jedi Council

After battling Grievous's droids, Anakin, Obi-Wan, and Palpatine make a fiery descent onto Coruscant in Grievous's badly damaged ship. Anakin is greeted by his wife, Padmé, who tells him that she has wonderful news: they are going to have a baby. Although she worries that this will make it difficult to keep their relationship secret any longer, Anakin comforts her, saying, "This is a happy moment—the happiest moment of my life."[2] Later that night, however, Anakin dreams that Padmé dies in childbirth. He resolves not to let the dream come true.

Soon afterward, Chancellor Palpatine appoints Anakin to serve as his personal representative on the Jedi Council. Although the Jedi agree to allow Anakin to sit on the Council, they do not grant him the rank of master. Anakin is outraged, but Obi-Wan tries to soothe him, saying no one his age has ever

been on the Council before. He also asks Anakin to spy on the chancellor for the Jedi, a move that Anakin believes is treasonous and against the Jedi way.

Anakin and Padmé keep their relationship a secret.

The Sith Lord

Later, Anakin meets with Palpatine, who tells
him that he has discovered Grievous's location and
that he hopes the Jedi Council will send Anakin
personally to destroy Grievous. Then he relates the
legend of Darth Plagueis, a Sith Lord so powerful
that he could keep his loved ones from dying.
He tells Anakin, "The dark side of the Force is
a pathway to many abilities some consider to be
unnatural."[3] Anakin is intrigued and wants to know
if it is possible to learn this power to defeat death;
the chancellor says that it will not be taught by a
Jedi.

Despite the chancellor's request that Anakin
be sent to deal with Grievous, the Jedi Council
sends the more experienced Obi-Wan. He locates
Grievous on the planet Utapau, where he destroys
the droid commander after a long battle.

Meanwhile, on Coruscant, Palpatine plays on
Anakin's wavering faith in the Jedi, telling the
young man that the other Jedi do not trust him
because they sense that he will be more powerful
than any of them. He reveals to Anakin that he
knows the dark side of the Force and says that he
can teach Anakin how to use it to keep his wife

from dying. Suddenly recognizing that Palpatine is a Sith Lord, Anakin pulls his lightsaber. Rather than killing Palpatine as he says he would like to do, he decides to turn him over to the Jedi Council.

Darth Vader

Anakin brings the information of Palpatine's true identity to Mace Windu and offers to help arrest the Sith Lord. Windu, however, senses confusion in the young man and tells him to remain in the Council chambers until Palpatine has been captured. While waiting there, Anakin hears Palpatine's voice come to him through the Force, saying that if he is destroyed, the only way to save Padmé will be lost. Crying, Anakin makes his decision: he races to the chancellor's office, where Windu has Palpatine cornered. Palpatine shoots Force Lightning from his hands, but Windu deflects it back at the Sith Lord, deforming his face. Although Palpatine begs for his life, Windu prepares to kill him, overriding Anakin's protest that it is not the Jedi way by saying that Palpatine is too dangerous to live. Anakin intervenes, cutting off Windu's arm and enabling Palpatine to kill the Jedi master. Although Anakin cannot believe what he has done, Palpatine tells him, "You're fulfilling your destiny, Anakin. . . . Become my apprentice. Learn to use the dark side of the Force."[4] Anakin agrees, as long as Palpatine promises to help him save Padmé, and the Sith Lord renames his new apprentice Darth Vader.

Palpatine immediately sends Anakin on a mission to destroy the Jedi at the temple and then to kill the Separatist leaders on the volcanic planet Mustafar. As Anakin carries out his orders, Palpatine issues Order 66 to the clones fighting alongside Obi-Wan, Yoda (who is aiding the Wookiees in battle), and the other Jedi against the Separatists. Order 66 is an order for the clones to turn against the Jedi and begin firing on them. Most of the Jedi are slaughtered, but Obi-Wan and Yoda manage to escape.

In the Senate on Coruscant, Palpatine accuses the Jedi of attempting to overthrow him and announces that the Republic will be reorganized into an Empire. His words are met with cheers, prompting Padmé to remark, "So this is how liberty dies, with thunderous applause."[5] Meanwhile, Obi-Wan discovers a security recording of Anakin cutting down the younglings in the Jedi temple. He reluctantly sets out to kill his former pupil, first

Chancellor
Palpatine

visiting Padmé, who refuses to believe that Anakin
has turned to the dark side.

After Obi-Wan leaves, Padmé flies to Mustafar,
where she pleads with Anakin to turn away from

the dark side. Suddenly, Obi-Wan, who has secretly stowed away on Padmé's ship, appears behind her. Believing that his wife has betrayed him, Anakin uses the Force to strangle her, releasing his hold (and leaving her unconscious) to do battle with Obi-Wan. Meanwhile, Yoda fights Palpatine in the Senate chambers on Coruscant but fails to defeat the Sith Lord and retreats.

Back on Mustafar, Anakin and Obi-Wan duel with lightsabers as lava erupts around them. Eventually, their fight is carried into a river of lava, where they balance precariously on debris and droids. Obi-Wan manages to jump free of the lava onto the bank, but when Anakin tries to do so also, his old mentor slices off his legs and remaining arm. Anakin slides down the bank to the edge of the lava, where his cloak starts on fire. Soon his body is consumed by flames. Obi-Wan walks away, leaving him to die. However, the flames go out, and Palpatine arrives to rescue Anakin.

Obi-Wan transports Padmé to Bail Organa's ship, where she gives birth to twins. She names the babies Luke and Leia, then dies. According to the medical droids attending her, she has lost the will to live.

Having undergone his own painful operation, Anakin is raised from the table, now cloaked in the familiar black armor, helmet, and mask of the villain of *Episodes IV*, *V*, and *VI*. He takes a few raspy, mechanical breaths, then asks, in a new, deep voice, if his wife is safe. When Palpatine tells his new apprentice that he has killed Padmé in his own anger, Anakin yells in agony, and everything around him is destroyed.

In the film's final scenes, Luke and Leia, the last hope to save the galaxy from the Sith, are hidden. Leia is taken to live with Senator Bail Organa on Alderaan, while Luke will be raised by his aunt and uncle on Tatooine.

Anakin's sense of morality decreases as he becomes involved with the dark side.

How to Apply Moral Criticism to *Star Wars: Episode III Revenge of the Sith*

What Is Moral Criticism?

The word *moral* refers to whether an action is right or wrong. The rightness of an action is generally judged on the basis of a society's or group's moral code, or its rules of conduct. Moral criticism, therefore, looks for the moral values in a work of art. Although more often researched within the study of philosophy or ethics, moral criticism can be applied to film.

Before writing a moral critique, an author might ask several questions: Does the work represent certain actions as being right or wrong? Do its characters follow a specific moral code? What happens when they stray from it? The answer to these questions can help the critic identify the work's moral message.

Applying Moral Criticism to
Revenge of the Sith

For most viewers, the conclusion of *Star Wars: Episode III Revenge of the Sith* does not come as a surprise. Anyone who has seen the original *Star Wars* trilogy knows that the young Jedi Anakin Skywalker turns to the dark side and becomes Darth Vader. Indeed, it is not the fact that Anakin does transform, but *how* that transformation comes about that makes up the heart of this film. Ultimately, the dire consequences of Anakin's failure to live up to the Jedi code serve as a warning to struggle against the dark side of our own nature.

The Jedi live by a clear moral code, which Anakin knows and tries to uphold. Anakin has been indoctrinated into the Jedi way, which calls for patience, compassion, and control. Jedi are not to be angry or fearful, nor are they to become attached to another individual. At every turn, Anakin is reminded of this code by

> **Thesis Statement**
> The author gives the thesis statement in the first paragraph: "Ultimately, the dire consequences of Anakin's failure to live up to the Jedi code serve as a warning to struggle against the dark side of our own nature."

> **Argument One**
> The author begins to argue the thesis, focusing on the movie's moral foundation: "The Jedi live by a clear moral code, which Anakin knows and tries to uphold."

the others in the Jedi order, and the young man himself recites Jedi doctrine on many occasions. He is the one who advises patience when he, Obi-Wan, and Chancellor Palpatine are trapped in a ray shield on General Grievous's ship. When the Jedi request that Anakin spy on Chancellor Palpatine, he is taken aback, telling Obi-Wan, "You're asking me to do something against the Jedi code."[1] Although ultimately the Jedi are right to suspect Palpatine, Anakin is correct in his assessment that asking him to act deceptively is not in accord with the Jedi way. Even after killing Count Dooku, Anakin recognizes that giving in to his anger was against the Jedi's moral code: "[Dooku] was an unarmed prisoner. I shouldn't have done that. It's not the Jedi way."[2]

Despite his attempts to uphold the Jedi code, Anakin ultimately fails and gives in to the dark side. In secretly marrying Padmé and fathering her unborn children, Anakin has arrogantly set himself above the Jedi's rules. Anakin also often lets his anger overcome him, as when he lashes out at the Jedi Council after being told that he will not be made a Jedi master: "How can you do this? This

> **Argument Two**
> The second argument looks at how Anakin "fails and gives in to the dark side."

is outrageous. It's unfair."[3] Along with his arrogance and anger, Anakin allows himself to be ruled by fear. After having a nightmare vision of Padmé dying in childbirth, Anakin becomes terrified of losing her. When he confesses his vision (though not its subject) to Yoda, the Jedi master councils him, "Train yourself to let go of everything you fear to lose."[4] Yet, rather than letting go, Anakin vows to find a way to save his wife. Thus, when Chancellor Palpatine tells Anakin that he can help save Padmé, the young Jedi faces an internal struggle: he now knows that Palpatine is a Sith Lord—a representative of all that he has been charged to fight against—but he also believes that Palpatine is the only one who can show him how to save his wife.

In the end, his fear of losing her wins out, and Anakin betrays his fellow Jedi Mace Windu, cutting off his arm and allowing Palpatine to kill him. Anakin pledges to become Darth Sidious's apprentice, telling the Sith Lord, "Just help me save Padmé's life. I can't live without her."[5] With that, Darth Sidious gives Anakin the new name Darth Vader, and a villain is born.

In the end, this turn to the dark side results in dire consequences to Anakin and to those he loves. The Jedi—who have taught and trained him since he was a young boy—are all but wiped out. His best friend and mentor, Obi-Wan, has no choice but to turn against him. Even more devastating, he loses Padmé. Even before she dies, Padmé is lost to Anakin, as she tells him that she cannot go down this path with him. Ironically, after working so hard to gain the power to save her, Anakin now uses that power to strangle her. Although he stops short of killing her, Anakin is still to blame for her death. She loses the will to live after realizing who Anakin has become. Ultimately, Anakin also loses his own humanity. He no longer has a functioning body of his own. Instead, he is encased in black armor. His deep voice and even his raspy breathing are controlled by a computer.

As an audience, we can identify with Anakin's experiences as well as his weaknesses. Throughout much of

> **Argument Three**
> In the third argument, the author focuses on the results of Anakin's downfall: "In the end, this turn to the dark side results in dire consequences to Anakin and to those he loves."

> **Argument Four**
> The final argument speaks to what viewers can take from the film: "As an audience, we can identify with Anakin's experiences as well as his weaknesses."

the film, Anakin is a sympathetic character. We can appreciate the fact that he wants to save Obi-Wan after the battle on Grievous's ship; we can relate to the anger at being passed over for a top spot on the Jedi Council; and we can even understand the willingness to do anything to keep a loved one from dying.

In the end, *Revenge of the Sith* presents a clear moral message: we can choose to be like Anakin, ignoring our moral code and giving in to the dark side, or we can follow that code and avoid the dehumanizing loss Anakin suffers. Even with its stark ending, the film's message is not all negative. Those viewers who go into this film already knowing that Anakin will become Darth Vader also know that by the end of the *Star Wars* saga, he will be redeemed by his love for his son, Luke. Although *Revenge of the Sith* may offer a bleak look at human weakness, the knowledge that even a villain can be redeemed makes one hope that those who fall from their moral code can eventually find their way back to the light side.

Conclusion
The final paragraph is the conclusion. It summarizes the arguments presented in the critique and partially restates the thesis.

Thinking Critically About *Revenge of the Sith*

Now it is your turn to assess the critique.
Consider these questions:

1. Do you think moral codes are always as clear-cut as the Jedi code? What kinds of moral codes do you see in the world today?

2. Do you think Anakin tries to follow the Jedi code? Or is he working against the code from the beginning of the film?

3. Can you see any of your own weaknesses in Anakin's character? Do you think the film serves as an effective warning against these weaknesses?

Other Approaches

What you have just read is one possible way to apply moral criticism to the film *Revenge of the Sith*. What are some other ways to apply this approach? Remember that moral criticism considers the moral message or ideas conveyed by a work. Following are two alternate approaches.

Condemnation of Individuality

Critic Tony Vinci sees Anakin's downfall in *Revenge of the Sith* as a critique of individuality, noting that throughout the prequel trilogy, Anakin is an autonomous character. He argues that Anakin's individualism develops into an egotistic drive for power and that eventually, even his most noble actions—such as rescuing Obi-Wan and attempting to save Padmé—are revealed to be "selfish desires for more power."[6]

A thesis for such a critique could be: *Revenge of the Sith* condemns individualism by showing that Anakin Skywalker's autonomy leads to a corrupting desire for power.

No Other Way

Some critics see Anakin Skywalker's fate as inevitable. Rather than a result of a calculated decision to turn to the dark side, they believe that Anakin is a victim of circumstances. He could not choose whether or not to fall in love with Padmé, nor could he help the fact that he was given such great power with the Force.

The thesis for a critique focusing on the inevitability of Anakin's fate might be: *Revenge of the Sith* reveals that whether we are on the light side or the dark side, circumstances beyond our control ultimately determine our fate.

You Critique It

Now that you have learned about several different critical theories and how to apply them to film, are you ready to perform a critique of your own? You have read that this type of evaluation can help you look at movies from a new perspective and make you pay attention to issues you may not have otherwise recognized. So, why not use one of the critical theories profiled in this book to consider a fresh take on your favorite movie?

First, choose a theory and the movie you want to analyze. Remember that the theory is a springboard for asking questions about the work.

Next, write a specific question that relates to the theory you have selected. Then you can form your thesis, which should provide the answer to that question. Your thesis is the most important part of your critique and offers an argument about the work based on the tenets, or beliefs, of the theory you are applying. Recall that the thesis statement typically appears at the very end of the introductory paragraph of your essay. It is usually only one sentence long.

After you have written your thesis, find evidence to back it up. Good places to start are in the work itself or journals or articles that discuss what other people have said about it. Since you are critiquing a movie, you may also want to read about the director's life to get a sense of what factors may have affected the creative process. This can be useful if working within historical or auteur types of criticism.

Depending on which theory you apply you can often find evidence in the movie's language, plot, or character development. You should also explore parts of the movie that seem to disprove your thesis and create an argument against them. As you do this, you might want to address what other critics have written about the movie. Their quotes may help support your claim.

Before you start analyzing a work, think about the different arguments made in this book. Reflect on how evidence supporting the thesis was presented. Did you find that some of the techniques used to back up the arguments were more convincing than others? Try these methods as you prove your thesis in your own critique.

When you are finished writing your critique, read it over carefully. Is your thesis statement understandable? Do the supporting arguments flow logically, with the topic of each paragraph clearly stated? Can you add any information that would present your readers with a stronger argument in favor of your thesis? Were you able to use quotes from the movie, as well as from other critics, to enhance your ideas?

Did you see the work in a new light?

Timeline

1944 George Lucas is born on May 14 in Modesto, California.

1962 On June 12, Lucas is in a near-fatal car accident.

1980 *The Empire Strikes Back* is released.

1981 Lucas and his wife adopt a baby girl, Amanda.

Raiders of the Lost Ark, produced by Lucas and based on a story he wrote, opens.

1983 *Return of the Jedi* is released, and Lucas and his wife divorce.

1984 *Indiana Jones and the Temple of Doom*, on which Lucas served as executive producer, opens.

1988 Lucas adopts a second daughter, Katie.

Lucas serves as executive producer on *Willow*, a fantasy based on his original story.

1989 Lucas is executive producer on *Indiana Jones and the Last Crusade*.

1992 Lucas is presented with the Irving G. Thalberg Award.

1993 Lucas adopts a son, Jett.

1966 Lucas graduates with a bachelor of arts in film from the University of Southern California on August 6.

1969 Lucas marries Marcia Griffin on February 22.

1971 THX 1138, Lucas's first feature-length film, is released to mixed reviews.

Lucas founds the film production company Lucasfilm.

1973 American Graffiti opens and becomes Lucas's first commercial success.

1977 Star Wars is released on May 25 and becomes an instant blockbuster.

1978 Star Wars receives Academy Awards for art direction-set decoration, sound, costume design, film editing, music-original score, and visual effects.

1999 The Phantom Menace, first of the Star Wars prequel trilogy, opens on May 19.

2002 Attack of the Clones opens.

2005 Revenge of the Sith opens.

2008 Lucas serves as executive producer on Indiana Jones and the Kingdom of the Crystal Skull.

2010 Lucas executive produces Red Tails, for which he wrote the story.

Glossary

ambivalence
>The presence of contradictory or conflicting attitudes or feelings about an object, person, or idea.

anthropology
>The study of humans, especially human cultures and development.

autonomous
>Independent; acting alone, and not controlled by others.

capitalism
>An economic system in which businesses are privately owned and compete with one another for profit.

clone
>An organism, such as a plant, animal, or person, that is produced from a single, parent organism and that has the identical genetic makeup to that parent.

contemporary
>Living during or coming from the same time period.

digital
>Having to do with a recording process that converts sounds and images into electronic signals to be stored or transmitted.

doctrine
>Beliefs held by a specific group, such as a religion.

hologram
>A three-dimensional image of an object produced using light.

imagery
>The use of images and figurative language in a literary work.

imperial
>Having to do with an empire or an emperor.

inflation
>An excessive or sustained increase in prices caused by an increase in the amount of money or credit available compared with the quantity of goods and services available.

prequel
>A movie or novel whose action takes place before that of a work that was released earlier.

separatist
>A person or group that supports breaking away from a larger body, such as an organization or country.

symbolism
>A literary and artistic technique in which ideas are conveyed through the use of symbols, or objects and events that stand for other, often abstract, ideas.

sympathetic
>Arousing feelings of sympathy or compassion.

Watergate
>A political scandal involving the 1972 government-directed burglary of the Democratic National Committee's headquarters, which resulted in the resignation of President Richard Nixon.

Bibliography of Works and Criticism

Important Works

THX 1138, 1971

American Graffiti, 1973

Star Wars: Episode IV A New Hope, 1977

Star Wars: Episode V The Empire Strikes Back, 1980

Raiders of the Lost Ark, 1981

Star Wars: Episode VI Return of the Jedi, 1983

Indiana Jones and the Temple of Doom, 1984

Howard the Duck, 1986

Willow, 1988

The Land Before Time, 1988

Indiana Jones and the Last Crusade, 1989

Radioland Murders, 1994

Star Wars: Episode I The Phantom Menace, 1999

Star Wars: Episode II Attack of the Clones, 2002

Star Wars: Episode III Revenge of the Sith, 2005

Indiana Jones and the Kingdom of the Crystal Skull, 2008

Red Tails, 2010

Critical Discussions

Decker, Kevin, and Jason Eberl, eds. *Star Wars and Philosophy: More Powerful Than You Can Possibly Imagine*. Chicago: Open Court, 2005. Print.

Decker, Mark. "They Want Unfreedom and One-Dimensional Thought? I'll Give Them Unfreedom and One-Dimensional Thought: George Lucas, *THX-1138*, and the Persistence of Marcusian Social Critique in *American Graffiti* and the *Star Wars* Films." *Extrapolation* 50.3 (2009): 417–441. Print.

Geraghty, Lincoln. "Creating and Comparing Myth in Twentieth-Century Science Fiction: *Star Trek* and *Star Wars*." *Literature Film Quarterly* 33.3 (2005): 191–200. Print.

Lancashire, Anne. "*The Phantom Menace*: Repetition, Variation, Integration." *Film Criticism* 24.3 (Spring 2000): 23–44. Print.

Silvio, Carl, and Tony Vinci, eds. *Culture, Identities and Technology in the* Star Wars *Films: Essays on the Two Trilogies*. Jefferson, NC: McFarland, 2007. Print.

Resources

Selected Bibliography

Baxter, John. *Mythmaker: The Life and Works of George Lucas*. New York: Avon, 1999. Print.

Decker, Kevin, and Jason Eberl, eds. *Star Wars and Philosophy: More Powerful Than You Can Possibly Imagine*. Chicago: Open Court, 2005. Print.

Hearn, Marcus. *The Cinema of George Lucas*. New York: Harry N. Abrams, 2005. Print.

Pollock, Dale. *Skywalking: The Life and Films of George Lucas*. New York: Harmony, 1983. Print.

Further Readings

Burstyn, Linda. *Making Movies: A Guide for Young Filmmakers*. Los Angeles: Artists Rights Foundation, 2001. Print.

Hamilton, John. *Screenplay*. Edina, MN: Abdo, 2009. Print.

Miles, Liz. *Writing a Screenplay*. Chicago: Raintree, 2010. Print.

Shields, Charles J. *George Lucas*. Philadelphia: Chelsea House, 2002. Print.

Web Links

To learn more about critiquing the films of George Lucas, visit ABDO Publishing Company online at **www.abdopublishing.com**. Web sites about the films of George Lucas are featured on our Book Links page. These links are routinely monitored and updated to provide the most current information available.

For More Information

Museum of Modern Film Library

11 West 53 Street, New York, NY 10019

212-708-9400

www.moma.org/explore/collection/film

The Film Library at the Museum of Modern Art houses more than 22,000 films representing every genre and time period. It also hosts film screenings.

Museum of the Moving Image

3601 35th Avenue, Astoria, NY 11106

718-784-0077

www.movingimage.us

With more than 125,000 artifacts reflecting the history and technology of the moving image, the museum reveals the processes involved in producing, marketing, and exhibiting film and television images.

Source Notes

Chapter 1. Introduction to Critiques
None

Chapter 2. A Closer Look at George Lucas

1. Dale Pollock. *Skywalking: The Life and Films of George Lucas*. New York: Harmony, 1983. Print. xvi.

2. Marcus Hearn. *The Cinema of George Lucas*. New York: Harry N. Abrams, 2005. Print. 177.

3. Kerry O'Quinn. "The George Lucas Saga." *George Lucas Interviews*. Jackson, MI: University Press of Mississippi, 1999. Print. 100.

Chapter 3. An Overview of *Star Wars: Episode IV A New Hope*

1. *Star Wars: Episode IV A New Hope*. Dir. George Lucas. 20th Century Fox, 1977. DVD.

2. Ibid.

3. Ibid.

Chapter 4. How to Apply Historical Criticism to
Star Wars: Episode IV A New Hope

1. *Star Wars: Episode IV A New Hope*. Dir. George Lucas. 20th Century Fox, 1977. DVD.

2. Ibid.

3. Ibid.

4. Ibid.

5. Carl Silvio. "The *Star Wars* Trilogies and Global Capitalism." *Culture, Identities and Technology in the* Star Wars *Films: Essays on the Two Trilogies*. Jefferson, NC: McFarland, 2007. Print. 57.

Chapter 5. An Overview of *Star Wars: Episode I*
The Phantom Menace

1. *Star Wars: Episode I The Phantom Menace*. Dir. George Lucas. 20th Century Fox, 1999. DVD.

Chapter 6. How to Apply Feminist Criticism to
Star Wars: Episode I The Phantom Menace

1. *Star Wars: Episode I The Phantom Menace*. Dir. George Lucas. 20th Century Fox, 1999. DVD.

2. Ibid.

3. Ibid.

4. Ibid.

Source Notes Continued

Chapter 7. An Overview of *Star Wars: Episode II Attack of the Clones*

1. *Star Wars: Episode II Attack of the Clones*. Dir. George Lucas. 20th Century Fox, 2002. DVD.

2. Ibid.

Chapter 8. How to Apply New Criticism to *Star Wars: Episode II Attack of the Clones*

1. *Star Wars: Episode II Attack of the Clones*. Dir. George Lucas. 20th Century Fox, 2002. DVD.

2. Ibid.

3. Ibid.

4. Ibid.

5. Ibid.

6. Ibid.

7. Ibid.

8. William Stephens. "Stoicism in the Stars: Yoda, the Emperor, and the Force." *Star Wars and Philosophy: More Powerful Than You Can Possibly Imagine*. Chicago: Open Court, 2005. Print. 16.

Chapter 9. An Overview of *Star Wars: Episode III Revenge of the Sith*

1. *Star Wars: Episode III Revenge of the Sith*. Dir. George Lucas. 20th Century Fox, 2005. DVD.

2. Ibid.

3. Ibid.

4. Ibid.

5. Ibid.

Chapter 10. How to Apply Moral Criticism to *Star Wars: Episode III Revenge of the Sith*

1. *Star Wars: Episode III Revenge of the Sith*. Dir. George Lucas. 20th Century Fox, 2005. DVD.

2. Ibid.

3. Ibid.

4. Ibid.

5. Ibid.

6. Tony Vinci. "The Fall of the Rebellion; or, Defiant and Obedient Heroes in a Galaxy Far, Far Away: Individualism and Intertextuality in the *Star Wars* Trilogies." *Culture, Identities and Technology in the* Star Wars *Films: Essays on the Two Trilogies*. Jefferson, NC: McFarland, 2007. Print. 28.

Index

About the Author

Valerie Bodden has written more than 100 children's nonfiction books. She lives in Wisconsin with her family.

Photo Credits

Matt Sayles/AP Images, cover, 3; Arash Radpour/AP Images, 12, 99; AP Images, 17, 98; Lucasfilm Ltd./Twentieth Century Fox Film Corp./Photofest, 20, 25, 26, 30, 33; Lucasfilm Ltd./20th Century Fox/Photofest, 38, 41, 45, 46, 51, 56, 63, 64; Twentieth Century Fox/Photofest, 69; Lucasfilm Ltd./Photofest, 76, 79, 83, 86